ISBN 978-1-330-53890-6
PIBN 10075708

For support please visit www.forgottenbooks.com

1 MONTH OF
FREE
READING

at

www.ForgottenBooks.com

By purchasing this book you are eligible for one month membership to ForgottenBooks.com, giving you unlimited access to our entire collection of over 700,000 titles via our web site and mobile apps.

To claim your free month visit:

www.forgottenbooks.com/free75708

English
Français
Deutsche
Italiano
Español
Português

www.forgottenbooks.com

Mythology Photography **Fiction**
Fishing Christianity **Art** Cooking
Essays Buddhism Freemasonry
Medicine **Biology** Music **Ancient Egypt** Evolution Carpentry Physics
Dance Geology **Mathematics** Fitness
Shakespeare **Folklore** Yoga Marketing
Confidence Immortality Biographies
Poetry **Psychology** Witchcraft
Electronics Chemistry History **Law**
Accounting **Philosophy** Anthropology
Alchemy Drama Quantum Mechanics
Atheism Sexual Health **Ancient History**
Entrepreneurship Languages Sport
Paleontology Needlework Islam
Metaphysics Investment Archaeology
Parenting Statistics Criminology
Motivational

KIDNAPPED IN LONDON

Being the Story of my

CAPTURE BY,

DETENTION AT,
AND
RELEASE FROM

The Chinese Legation, London

BY

SUN YAT SEN

BRISTOL
J. W. ARROWSMITH, 11 QUAY STREET
LONDON
SIMPKIN, MARSHALL, HAMILTON, KENT AND COMPANY LIMITED
1897

CONTENTS.

PREFACE.

———

MY recent detention in the Chinese Legation, 49 Portland Place, London, has excited so much interest, has brought me so many friends and has raised so many legal, technical and international points of law, that I feel I should be failing in my duty did I not place on public record, all the circumstances connected with the historical event.

I must beg the indulgence of all readers for my shortcomings in English composition, and confess that had it not been for the help rendered by a good friend, who transcribed my thoughts, I could never have ventured to appear as the Author of an English book.

SUN YAT SEN.

LONDON, 1897.

Kidnapped in London.

CHAPTER I.

THE IMBROGLIO.

WHEN in 1892 I settled in Macao, a small island near the mouth of the Canton river, to practise medicine, I little dreamt that in four years time I should find myself a prisoner in the Chinese Legation in London, and the unwitting cause of a political sensation which culminated in the active interference of the British Government to procure my release. It was in that year however, and at Macao, that my first acquaintance was

9

made with political life ; and there began the part of my career which has been the means of bringing my name so prominently before the British people.

I had been studying medicine, during the year 1886, in Canton at the Anglo-American Mission, under the direction of the venerable Dr. Kerr, when in 1887 I heard of the opening of a College of Medicine at Hong Kong, and determined immediately to avail myself of the advantages it offered.

After five years' study (1887—1892) I obtained the diploma entitling me to style myself " Licentiate in Medicine and Surgery, Hong Kong."

Macao has belonged to Portugal for 360 years ; but although the Government is Europeanised, the inhabitants are mostly Chinese, and the section of the population which styles itself Portuguese, consists really of Eurasians of several in-bred generations.

In my newly selected home, I found the Chinese authorities of the native hospital willing to help me forward in the matter of affording me opportunities to practise European medicine and surgery. They placed a ward at my disposal, supplied me with drugs and appliances from London, and granted me every privilege whereby to secure my introduction amongst them on a fair footing.

This event deserves special notice as marking a new and significant departure in China ; for never before had the Board of Directors of any Chinese hospital throughout the length and breadth of the great empire given any direct official encouragement to Western medicine. Many patients, more especially surgical cases, came to my wards, and I had the opportunity of performing several of the major operations before the Directors. On the other hand, I had difficulty from the first with the Portuguese authorities.

It was not the obstructive ignorance of the East, but the jealousy of the West, which stepped in to thwart my progress. The law of Portugal forbids the practice of medicine, within Portuguese territory, by any one who is not possessed of a Portuguese diploma, obtainable only in Europe. Under this rule the Portuguese doctors took refuge and fought my claims to practise. They first forbade me to practise amongst, or prescribe for, Portuguese; the dispensers in the pharmacies were not allowed to dispense prescriptions from the pen of a doctor of any alien nationality; consequently my progress was hampered from the first. After futile attempts to establish myself in Macao, and at considerable pecuniary loss, for I had settled down little dreaming of opposition, I was induced to go to Canton.

It was in Macao that I first learned of the existence of a political movement which I might best describe as the formation of a " Young China " party. Its objects were so wise, so modest, and so hopeful, that my sympathies were at once enlisted in its behalf, and I believed I was doing my best to further the interests of my country by joining it. The idea was to bring about a peaceful reformation, and we hoped, by forwarding modest schemes of reform to the Throne, to initiate a form of government more consistent with modern requirements. The prime essence of the movement was the establishment of a form of constitutional government to supplement the old-fashioned, corrupt, and worn-out system under which China is groaning.

It is unnecessary to enter into details as to what form of rule obtains in China at present. It may be summed up, however, in a few words. The people have no say whatever in the management of Imperial, National, or even Municipal affairs. The mandarins, or local magistrates, have full power of adjudication, from which there is no appeal. Their word is law, and they have full scope to practise their machinations with complete irresponsibility, and every officer may fatten himself with impunity. Extortion by officials is an institution ; it is the condition on which they take office ; and it is only when the bleeder is a bungler that the government steps in with pretended benevolence to ameliorate but more often to complete the depletion.

English readers are probably unaware of the smallness of the established salaries of provincial magnates. They will scarcely credit that the Viceroy of, say, Canton, ruling a country with a population larger than that of Great Britain, is allowed as his legal salary the paltry sum of £60 a year ; so that, in order to live and maintain himself in office, accumulating fabulous riches the while, he resorts to extortion and the selling of justice.

So-called education and the results of examinations are the one means of obtaining official notice. Granted that a young scholar gains distinction, he proceeds to seek public employment, and, by bribing the Peking authorities, an official post is hoped for. Once obtained, as he cannot live on his salary, perhaps he even pays so much annually for his post, licence to squeeze is the result, and the man must be stupid indeed who cannot, when backed up by government, make himself rich enough to buy a still higher post in a few years. With advancement comes increased licence and additional facility for self-enrichment, so that the cleverest " squeezer " ultimately can obtain money enough to purchase the highest positions.

This official thief, with his mind warped by his mode of life, is the ultimate authority in all matters of social, political, and criminal life. It is a feudal system,

an *imperium in imperio*, an unjust auto-
cracy, which thrives by its own rottenness.
But this system of fattening on the public
vitals—the selling of power—is the chief
means by which the Manchu dynasty
continues to exist. With this legalised
corruption stamped as the highest ideal
of government, who can wonder at the
existence of a strong undercurrent of
dissatisfaction among the people ?

The masses of China, although kept
officially in ignorance of what is going on
in the world around them, are anything
but a stupid people. All European authorities on this matter state that the
latent intellectual ability of the Chinese
is considerable ; and many place it even
above that of the masses in any other
country, European or Asiatic. Books on
politics are not allowed ; daily newspapers
are prohibited in China ; the world around,
its people and politics, are shut out ; while
no one below the grade of a mandarin of

the seventh rank is allowed to read Chinese geography, far less foreign. The laws of the present dynasty are *not* for public reading ; they are known only to the highest officials. The reading of books on military subjects is, in common with that of other prohibited matter, not only forbidden, but is even punishable by death. No one is allowed, on pain of death, to invent anything new, or to make known any new discovery. In this way are the people kept in darkness, while the government doles out to them what scraps of information it finds will suit its own ends.

The so-called " Literati " of China are allowed to study only the Chinese classics and the commentaries thereon. These consist of the writings of ancient philosophers, the works of Confucius and others. But of even these, all parts relating to the criticism of their superiors are carefully expunged, and only those parts are published for public reading which teach obedience to authorities as the essence of all instruction. In this way is China ruled—or rather misruled—namely, by the enforcement of blind obedience to all existing laws and formalities.

To keep the masses in ignorance is the constant endeavour of Chinese rule. In this way it happened, that during the last Japanese incursion, absolutely nothing was known of the war by the masses of China, in parts other than those where the campaign was actually waged. Not only did the people a short way inland never hear of the war, but the masses had never even heard of a people called Japanese; and even where the whisper had been echoed, it was discussed as being a " rebellion " of the " foreign man."

With this incubus hanging over her, China has no chance of reform except it come from the Throne; and it was to induce the Throne to modify this pernicious state of things that the " Young China " party was formed. Hoping that the Peking authorities, by their more extended contact during recent years with foreign diplomatists, might have learned something of constitutional rule, and might be willing to aid the people in throwing off their deplorable ignorance, I ventured, with others, to approach them, beseeching them, in all humility, to move in this direction for the welfare of China. These petitions only resulted in the infliction of many rigorous punishments. We had seized the moment when the Japanese were threatening Peking, and the Emperor, fearing that harsh dealings with the reformers might alienate many of his people, took no notice of them until peace was assured. Then an edict was issued denouncing the petitioners and commanding the immediate cessation of all suggestions of reform.

Finding the door closed to mild means, we grew more concrete in our notions and demands, and gradually came to see that some degree of coercion would be necessary. In all quarters we found supporters. The better classes were dissatisfied with the behaviour of our armies and fleets, and knew that corruption in its worst forms was the cause of their failure. This feeling was not confined to one locality, but was wide-spread and deep-rooted, and promised to take shape and find expression in decided action.

The headquarters of the "Young China" party was really in Shanghai, but the scene of action was to be laid in Canton. The party was aided in its course by one or two circumstances. First among these was the existence of discontented soldiery. Three-fourths of the Cantonese contingent were disbanded when the war in the North had ceased in 1895. This set loose a number of idle, lawless men; and the small section of their comrades who were retained in service were no better pleased than those dismissed. Either disband all or retain all, was their cry; but the authorities were deaf to the remonstrance. The reform party at once enlisted the sympathies of these men in their cause, and so gained numerical strength to their military resources.

Another chance coincidence hastened events. For some reason or other a body of police, discarding their uniform, set to work to loot and plunder a section of the city. After an hour or two, the inhabitants rose, and obtaining mastery of the quondam police, shut some half-dozen of the ringleaders up in their Guildhall. The superintendent of the official police then sent out a force to release the marauders, and proceeded forthwith to plunder the Guildhall itself. A meeting of the inhabitants was immediately held, and a deputation of 1000 men sent to the Governor's residence to appeal against the action of the police. The authorities, however, told the deputation that such a proceeding was tantamount to a rebellion, and that they had no right to threaten their superiors. They thereupon arrested the ringleaders of the deputation, and sent the others about their business The discontents soon became disaffected, and, the " Young China " party making advances, they readily joined the reformers.

Yet a third and a fourth incident helped to swell their ranks. The Viceroy, Li Han Chang (brother of the famous Viceroy Li), put a fixed tariff on all official posts throughout his two provinces, Kwang-Tung and Kwang-Si. This was an innovation which meant a further " squeeze " of the people, as the officials, of course, made the people pay to indemnify them for their extra payments. The fourth, and the most characteristically Chinese method of extortion was afforded in the occasion of the Viceroy's birthday. The officials in his provinces combined to give their master a present, and collected money to the amount of a million taels (about £200,000). Of course the officials took the money from the richer merchants in the usual way, by threats, by promises, and by blackmailing. A follower of Li Han Chang, Che Fa Nung by name, further angered all the " Literati " by selling, to all who could afford to pay, diplomas of graduation for 3000 taels (about £500) each. The richer men and the " Literati " became thereby disaffected and threw in their lot with " Young China."

In this way the reform movement acquired great strength and coherence and wide-spread influence, and brought matters all too soon to a climax. The plan was to capture the city of Canton and depose the authorities, taking them by surprise and securing them in as quiet a way as possible, or, at any rate, without bloodshed. To ensure a complete *coup*, it was considered necessary to bring an overwhelming force to bear ; consequently, two bodies of men were employed, one in Swatow and the other from the banks of the West river. These places were fixed upon as the Swatow men, for instance, were totally ignorant of the Cantonese language. Although only 180 miles north of Canton, the language of Swatow differs as much from that of Canton as English does from Italian. It was deemed wise to bring strangers in, as they were more likely to be staunch to the cause, since they could not communicate with, and therefore could not be tampered with by, Cantonese men. Nor would it be safe for them to disband or desert, as they would be known as strangers, and suspicion would at once fall on them were they found in Canton after the disturbance.

It was arranged that on a certain day in October, 1895, these men should march across country, one body from the south-

west, the other from the north-east, towards
Canton. All proceeded satisfactorily, and
they commenced their advance. Frequent
meetings of the Committee of Reformers
were held, and arms, ammunition and
dynamite were accumulated at the headquarters. The soldiers advancing across
the country were to be still further
strengthened by a contingent of four
hundred men from Hong Kong. The
day for the assemblage came and the
southern men were halted within four
hours march of the city. A guard of one
hundred men, fully armed, was stationed
around the Committee in their Guild;
runners, some thirty in number, were
despatched to the disaffected over the
city to be ready for the following morning.
Whilst the conspirators sat within their
hall a telegram was received to the effect
that the advancing soldiers had been
stayed in their progress, and the reform
movement forthwith became disconcerted.

It was impossible to recall the messengers, and others could not be found who knew where the disaffected were resident. Further news came to hand rendering it impossible to proceed, and the cry arose " *Sauvé qui peut.*"   A general stampede followed; papers were burnt, arms hidden, and telegrams despatched to Hong Kong to stop the contingent from that place. The telegram to the Hong Kong agent, however, only reached him after all his men had been got on board a steamer, which also carried many barrels of revolvers.   Instead of dismissing the men as he should have done, he allowed them to proceed, and they landed on the wharf of Canton only to find themselves placed under arrest.   The leaders in Canton fled, some one way, some another; I myself, after several hairbreadth escapes, getting on board a steam launch in which I sailed to Macao.   Remaining there for twenty-four hours only, I proceeded to

Hong Kong, where, after calling on some friends, I sought my old teacher and friend, Mr. James Cantlie. Having informed him that I was in trouble through having offended the Cantonese authorities, and fearing that I should be arrested and sent to Canton for execution, he advised me to consult a lawyer, which I immediately proceeded to do.

CHAPTER II.

MY CAPTURE.

I DID not see Mr. Cantlie again, as Mr. Dennis, who directed my steps, constrained me to get away at once.

In two days time I went by Japanese steamer to Kobe, whence, after a few days' stay, I proceeded to Yokohama. There I changed my Chinese attire for a European costume *à la* Japanese. I removed my queue, allowed my hair to grow naturally and cultivated my moustache. In a few days I sailed from Yokohama for the Hawaiian Islands and there took up my quarters in the town of Honolulu, where I had many relations, friends and well-wishers. Wherever I went, whether in Japan, Honolulu, or

America, I found all intelligent Chinese imbued with the spirit of reform and eager to obtain a form of representative government for their native land.

Whilst walking in the streets of Honolulu I met Mr. and Mrs. Cantlie and family, who were then on their way to England. They did not at first recognise me in my European dress, and their Japanese nurse at once addressed me in the Japanese language, taking me for a countryman. This happened frequently, Japanese everywhere at first taking me for one of themselves and only finding their mistake when they spoke to me.

I left Honolulu in June, 1896, for San Francisco, where I remained for a month before proceeding eastward. There I met many of my countrymen and was well received by them. I spent three months in America, and came to Liverpool by the s.s. *Majestic*   In New York I was advised to beware the Chinese

Minister to the United States, as he is a Manchurian, and has but little sympathy with Chinese generally and a reformer in particular.

On October 1st, 1896, I arrived in London and put up at Haxell's Hotel in the Strand.   I went next day to Mr. Cantlie's, at 46 Devonshire Street, Portland Place, W., where I received a hearty welcome from my old friend and his wife. Lodgings were found for me at 8 Gray's Inn Place, Gray's Inn, Holborn.   Henceforward I proceeded to settle down to enjoy my stay in London and to become acquainted with the many sights, the museums and the historical relics in this the very centre of the universe   What impressed me, a Chinaman, most was the enormous vehicular traffic, the endless and unceasing stream of omnibusses, cabs, carriages, wagons, and wheeled conveyances of humbler character which held the streets; the wonderful way in which the police controlled and directed the traffic, and the good humour of the people. The foot passengers are, of course, many, but they are not in such crowds as we find in Chinese streets. For one thing, our streets are much narrower, being, in fact, mere alleys; and, in the second place, all our goods are conveyed by human carriage, everything being slung from a bamboo pole carried across the shoulders Yet even in the wide streets of Hong Kong our foot passenger traffic is in swarms.

I was just beginning to know Holborn from the Strand, and Oxford Circus from Piccadilly Circus, when I was deprived of my liberty in the fashion so fully described by the public press of the country.

I had been frequently at Mr. Cantlie's, almost daily in fact, and spent most of my time in his study. One day at luncheon he alluded to the Chinese Lega- tion being in the neighbourhood, and jokingly suggested that I might go round and call there ; whereat his wife remarked, " You had better not.   Don't you go near it ; they 'll catch you and ship you off to China."   We all enjoyed a good laugh over the remark, little knowing how true the womanly instinct was, and how soon we were to experience the reality.   While dining one evening at Dr. Manson's, whom I had also known in Hong Kong, as my teacher in medicine, I was jokingly advised by him also to keep away from the Chinese Legation.   I was well warned, therefore ; but as I did not know where the Legation was, the warning was of little use.   I knew that to get to Devonshire Street I had to get off the omnibus at Oxford Circus, and from thence go straight north up a wide street till I found the name Devonshire on the corner house.   That was the extent of my knowledge of the locality at this time.

On Sunday morning, October 11th, at

almost half-past ten, I was walking towards Devonshire Street, hoping to be in time to go to church with the doctor and his family, when a Chinaman approached in a surreptitious manner from behind and asked, in English, whether I was Japanese or Chinese. I replied, " I am Chinese." He then inquired from what province I came, and when I told him I was from Canton he said, " We are countrymen, and speak the same language; I am from Canton." It should be observed that English or " Pidgin," that is " business " English, is the common language between Chinamen from different localities. A Swatow and a Cantonese merchant, although their towns are but 180 miles apart (less than the distance between London and Liverpool), may be entirely ignorant of each other's spoken language. The written language is the same all over China, but the written and spoken languages are totally different, and the spoken languages are many.　A Swatow merchant, therefore, doing business in Hong Kong with a Cantonese man, speaks English, but writes in the common language of China.　While upon this subject it may be well to state that the Japanese written language is the same in its characters as that used by the Chinese ; so that a Chinaman and a Japanese when they meet, although having no spoken words in common, can figure to each other on the ground or on paper, and frequently make imaginary figures on one hand with the forefinger of the other to their mutual understanding.

My would-be Chinese friend, therefore, addressed me in English until he found my dialect.　We then conversed in the Cantonese dialect.　Whilst he was talking we were slowly advancing along the street, and presently a second Chinaman joined us, so that I had now one on each side.　They pressed me to go in to their

" lodgings " and enjoy a smoke and chat with them. I gently demurred, and we stopped on the pavement. A third Chinaman now appeared and my first acquaintance left us. The two who remained further pressed me to accompany them, and I was gradually, and in a seemingly friendly manner, led to the upper edge of the pavement, when the door of an adjacent house suddenly opened and I was half-jokingly and half-persistently compelled to enter by my companions, one on either side, who rein-forced their entreaties by a quasi-friendly push. Suspecting nothing, for I knew not what house I was entering, I only hesitated because of my desire to get to Mr. Cantlie's in time for church, and I felt I should be too late did I delay. However, in good faith I entered, and was not a little surprised when the front door was somewhat hurriedly closed and barred behind me. All at once it flashed

upon me that the house must be the
Chinese Legation, thereby accounting for
the number of Chinamen in mandarin
attire, and for the large size of the house;
while I also recollected that the Minister
resided somewhere in the neighbourhood
of Devonshire Street, near to which I
must then be.

I was taken to a room on the ground
floor whilst one or two men talked to me
and to each other.   I was then sent
upstairs, two men, one on either side,
conducting and partly forcing me to as-
cend.   I was next shown into a room on
the second floor and told I was to remain
there.   This room, however, did not seem
to satisfy my captors, as I was shortly
afterwards taken to another on the third
floor with a barred window looking out to
the back of the house   Here an old
gentleman with white hair and beard
came into the room in rather a bumptious
fashion and said:

"Here is China for you; you are now in China."

Sitting down, he proceeded to interrogate me.

Asked what my name was, I replied "Sun."

"Your name," he replied, "is Sun Wen; and we have a telegram from the Chinese Minister in America informing us that you were a passenger to this country by the s.s. *Majestic*; and the Minister asks me to arrest you."

"What does that mean?" I enquired.

To which he replied:

"You have previously sent in a petition for reform to the Tsung-Li-Yamen in Peking asking that it be presented to the Emperor. That may be considered a very good petition; but now the Tsung-Li-Yamen want you, and therefore you are detained here until we learn what the Emperor wishes us to do with you."

"Can I let my friend know I am here ? "
I asked.

"No," he replied; "but you can write
to your lodging for your luggage to be
sent you."

On my expressing a wish to write to
Dr. Manson, he provided me with pen,
ink and paper. I wrote to Dr. Manson
informing him that I was confined in
the Chinese Legation, and asking him
to tell Mr. Cantlie to get my baggage sent
to me.   The old gentleman, however,—
whom I afterwards learned to be Sir
Halliday Macartney,—objected to my
using the word "confined," and asked
me to substitute another.   Accordingly I
wrote: "I am in the Chinese Legation;
please tell Mr. Cantlie to send my luggage
here."

He then said he did not want me to
write to my friend, and asked me to write
to my hotel.   I informed him that I
was not at a hotel, and that only Mr.

Cantlie knew where I was living.   It was
very evident my interrogator was playing
a crafty game to get hold of my effects,
and more especially my papers, in the
hope of finding correspondence whereby
to ascertain who my Chinese accomplices
or correspondents were.   I handed him
the letter to Dr. Manson, which he read
and returned, saying, " That is all right."
I put it in an envelope and gave it to Sir
Halliday Macartney in all good faith that
it would be delivered.

CHAPTER III.

MY IMPRISONMENT.

SIR HALLIDAY then left the room, shut the door and locked it, and I was a prisoner under lock and key. Shortly afterwards I was disturbed by the sound of carpentry at the door of my room, and found that an additional lock was being fixed thereto. Outside the door was stationed a guard of never less than two people, one of whom was a European; sometimes a third guard was added. During the first twenty-four hours the Chinese guards at the door frequently came in and spoke to me in their own dialect, which I understood fairly well. They did not give me any information as to my imprisonment—nor did I ask them any questions—further than that the old gentleman who had locked me up was Sir Halliday Macartney, the Ma-Ta-Yen, as they called him : *Ma* standing for " Macartney," *Ta-Yen* being the equivalent for " His Excellency." This is in the same category with the name under which the Chinese Minister passes here, Kung-Ta-Yen. *Kung* is his family name or surname; *Ta-Yen* indicates his title, meaning " His Excellency." He never gives his real name in public matters, thereby compelling every foreigner to unconsciously style him " His Excellency." I often wonder if he deals with the British Government under this cognomen solely; if he does, it is a disparagement and slight that is meant. Court and diplomatic etiquette in China is so nice, that the mere inflection of a syllable is quite enough to change the meaning of any communi cation to the foreigner from a compliment to a slight. This is constantly striven after in all dealings with foreigners, and it requires a very good knowledge of Chinese literature and culture indeed, to know that any message delivered to a foreigner does not leave the Chinese diplomatist hugging himself with delight at having insulted a foreigner of high rank, without his knowing it. To the people around him he thereby shows his own preëminence, and how the "foreign devils"—the Yang Quei Tze— are his inferiors.

Several hours after my imprisonment, one of the guard came into my room and told me that Sir Halliday Macartney had ordered him to search me. He proceeded to take my keys, pencil and knife. He did not find my pocket in which I had a few bank notes; but he took the few unimportant papers I had. They asked me what food I wanted, and at my request brought me some milk which I drank.

During the day two English servants came to light the fire, bring coals and sweep the room. I asked the first who came to take a letter out for me, and being promised that this would be done, I wrote a note addressed to Mr. Cantlie, 46 Devonshire Street, W. When the second servant came I did the same thing. I did not, of course, know till later what had happened to my letters, but both men said they had sent them. That (Sunday) evening an English woman came in to make up my bed. I did not address her at all. All that night I had no sleep, and lay with my clothes on.

On the following day—Monday, 12th October—the two English servants came again to attend to the room, and brought coals, water and food. One said he had sent the note with which I had entrusted him, while the other, Cole, said he could not get out to do so. I suspected, however, that my notes had never reached their destination.

On Tuesday, the 13th, I again asked

the younger manservant—not Cole—if he had delivered my letter and had seen Mr. Cantlie. He said he had; but as I still doubted him, he swore he had seen Mr. Cantlie, who on receiving the note said, " All right ! " Having no more paper, I wrote with pencil on the corner of my handkerchief, and asked him to take it to my friend. At the same time I put a half-sovereign in his hand, and hoped for the best. I was dubious about his good faith, and I found that my suspicions were but too well-founded ; for I ascertained subsequently he went immediately to his employers and disclosed all.

On the fourth day of my imprisonment Mr. Tang, as he is called, came to see me, and I recognised in him the man who had kidnapped me. He sat down and proceeded to converse with me.

" When I last saw you," he began, "and took you in here, I did so as part of my official duty : I now come to talk with

you as a friend. You had better confess
that you are Sun Wen; it is no use denying it: everything is settled." In a vein
of sarcastic-pseudo flattery he continued ·
"You are well known in China: the
Emperor and the Tsung-Li-Yamen are
well acquainted with your history; it is
surely worth your while dying with so
distinguished a name as you have made
for yourself upon you." (This is a species
of Oriental flattery scarcely perhaps to be
appreciated by Western minds; but it is
considered everything in China, how and
under what name and reputation you *die*.)
"Your being here," he proceeded, "means
life or death. Do you know that ?"

"How ?" I asked. "This is England,
not China. What do you propose to do
with me? If you wish extradition, you
must let my imprisonment be known to
the British Government; and I do not
think the Government of this country will
give me up."

"We are not going to ask legal extradition for you," he replied. "Everything is ready; the steamer is engaged; you are to be bound and gagged and taken from here, so that there will be no disturbance; and you will be placed on board in safe keeping. Outside Hong Kong harbour there will be a Chinese gunboat to meet you, and you will be transferred to that and taken to Canton for trial and execution."

I pointed out that this would be a risky proceeding, as I might have the chance of communicating with the English on board on the way. This, however, Tang declared would be impossible, as, said he, "You will be as carefully guarded as you are here, so that all possibility of escape will be cut off." I then suggested that the officers on board might not be of the same mind as my captors, and that some of them might sympathise with me and help me.

"The steamboat company," replied

Tang, "are friends of Sir Halliday Macartney's and will do what they are told."

In reply to my questions he told me that I should be taken by one of the "Glen" Line of Steamers, but that my departure would not take place that week (this was October 14th), as the Minister was unwilling to go to the expense of exclusively chartering the steamer, and he wished to have the cargo shipped first, so that only the passenger tickets would have to be paid for.

"Some time next week," he added, "the cargo will be embarked and you will go then."

On my remarking that this was a very difficult plan to put into execution, he merely said:

"Were we afraid of that, we could kill you here, because this is China, and no one can interfere with us in the Legation."

For my edification and consolation he

then quoted the case of a Korean patriot, who, escaping from Korea to Japan, was induced by a countryman of his to go to Shanghai, where he was put to death in the British concession. His dead body was sent back by the Chinese to Korea for punishment, and on arrival there it was decapitated, while the murderer was rewarded and given a high political post. Tang was evidently fondly cherishing the belief that he would be similarly promoted by his government for arresting me and securing my death.

I asked him why he should be so cruel, to which he replied:

" This is by order of the Emperor, who wants you captured at any price, alive or dead."

I urged that the Korean case was one of the causes of the Japanese war, and that my capture and execution might lead to further trouble and great complications.

" The British Government," I said,

"may ask for the punishment of all the members of this Legation; and, as you are a countryman of mine, my people in the province of Kwang-Tung may revenge themselves on you and your family for your treatment of me."

He then changed his tone, desisted from his arrogant utterances, and remarked that all he was doing was by the direction of the Legation, and that he was merely warning me in a friendly way of my plight.

CHAPTER IV

PLEADING WITH MY GAOLERS FOR LIFE.

AT twelve o'clock the same night Tang returned to my room and re-opened the subject. I asked him, if he was really a friend of mine, what he could do to help me.

"That is what I came back for," he replied, "and I want to do all I can, and will let you out by-and-by. Meantime," he continued, "I am getting the locksmith to make two duplicate keys, one for your room and one for the front door."

Tang had to take this step, he said, as the keys were kept by the confidential servant of the Minister, who would not part with them.

To my inquiry as to when he could let

me out, he stated that it would be impossible till the following day, and that he could probably manage it at two a.m. Friday morning.

As he left the room he counselled me to be ready to get out on the Friday.

After his departure I wrote down a few words on a paper to give to the servants to take to Mr. Cantlie.

Next morning, Thursday, October 15th, I gave the note to the servant; but, as Tang told me on the afternoon of that day, it was handed by the servant to the Legation authorities.

Tang declared that by my action I had spoiled all his plans for rescuing me, and that Sir Halliday Macartney had scolded him very much for telling me how they intended to dispose of me

I thereupon asked him if there was any hope for my life, to which he replied ·

" Yes, there is still great hope ; but you must do what I tell you."

He advised me to write to the Minister asking for mercy. This I agreed to do, and asked for pen, ink and paper. These Tang told Cole to bring me.

I asked, however, that Chinese ink and paper should be supplied me, as I could not write to the Chinese Minister in English.

To this Tang replied :

"Oh, English is best, for the Minister is but a figure-head; everything is in Macartney's hands, and you had better write to him."

When I asked what I should write, he said

"You must deny that you had anything to do with the Canton plot, declare that you were wrongly accused by the mandarins, and that you came to the Legation to ask for redress."

I wrote to his dictation a long letter to this effect in Tang's presence.

Having addressed the folded paper to

Sir Halliday Macartney (whose name Tang spelt for me, as I did not know how) I handed it to Tang, who went off with it in his possession, and I never saw the intriguer again.

This was no doubt a very stupid thing to have done, as I thereby furnished my enemies with documentary evidence that I had come voluntarily to the Legation. But as a dying man will clutch at anything, so I, in my strait, was easily imposed upon.

Tang had informed me that all my notes had been given up by the servants, so that none of them had reached my friends outside. I then lost all hope, and was persuaded that I was face to face with death.

During the week I had written statements of my plight on any scraps of paper I could get and thrown them out of the window. I had at first given them to the servants to throw out, as my window did not look out on the street; but it was evident all of them had been retained. I therefore attempted to throw them out at my own window myself, and by a lucky shot one fell on the leads of the back premises of the next house.

In order to make these missives travel further I weighted them with coppers, and, when these were exhausted, two-shilling pieces, which, in spite of the search, I had managed to retain on my person. When the note fell on the next house I was in hopes that the occupants might get it. One of the other notes, striking a rope, fell down immediately outside my window. I requested a servant—not Cole—to pick it up and give it me; but instead of doing so he told the Chinese guards about it, and they picked it up.

Whilst searching about, the letter on the leads of the next house caught their attention, and, climbing over, they got possession of that also, so that I was bereft of that hope too. These notes they took to their masters.

I was now in a worse plight than ever, for they screwed up my window, and my sole means of communication with the outside world seemed gone.

My despair was complete, and only by prayer to God could I gain any comfort. Still the dreary days and still more dreary nights wore on, and but for the comfort afforded me by prayer I believe I should have gone mad. After my release I related to Mr. Cantlie how prayer was my one hope, and told him how I should never forget the feeling that seemed to take possession of me as I rose from my knees on the morning of Friday, October 16th—a feeling of calmness, hopefulness and confidence, that assured me my prayer was heard, and filled me with hope that all would yet be well. I therefore resolved to redouble my efforts, and made a determined advance to Cole, beseeching him to help me.

When he came in I asked him : " Can you do anything for me ? "

His reply was the question : " What are you ? "

" A political refugee from China," I told him.

As he did not seem to quite grasp my meaning, I asked him if he had heard much about the Armenians. He said he had, so I followed up this line by telling him that just as the Sultan of Turkey wished to kill all the Christians of Armenia, so the Emperor of China wished to kill me because I was a Christian, and one of a party that was striving to secure good government for China.

" All English people," I said, " sympathise with the Armenians, and I do not doubt they would have the same feeling towards me if they knew my condition."

He remarked that he did not know whether the English Government would help me, but I replied that they would certainly do so, otherwise the Chinese Legation would not confine me so strictly, but would openly ask the British Government for my legal extradition.

" My life," I said to him, "is in your hands. If you let the matter be known outside, I shall be saved; if not, I shall certainly be executed. Is it good to save a life or to take it? Whether is it more important to regard your duty to God or to your master?—to honour the just British, or the corrupt Chinese, Government?"

I pleaded with him to think over what I had said, and to give me an answer next time he came, and tell me truly whether he would help me or not.

He went away, and I did not see him till next morning. It may well be imagined how eager I was to learn his decision.

While engaged putting coals on the fire he pointed to a paper he had placed in the coal scuttle. On the contents of that paper my life seemed to depend. Would it prove a messenger of hope, or would the door of hope again be shut in my face? Immediately he left the room I picked it up and read:

" I will try to take a letter to your friend. You must not write it at the table, as you can be seen through the keyhole, and the guards outside watch you constantly. You must write it on your bed."

I then lay down on my bed, with my face to the wall, and wrote on a visiting card to Mr. Cantlie. At noon Cole came in again, and I pointed to where my note was. He went and picked it up, and I gave him all the money I had about me— £20. Mr. Cantlie's note in reply was placed by Cole behind the coal scuttle, and by a significant glance he indicated there was something there for me. When he had gone I anxiously picked it up, and was overjoyed to read the words · " Cheer up ! The Government is working on your behalf, and you will be free in a few days." Then I knew God had answered my prayer.

During all this time I had never taken off my clothes. Sleep came but seldom, only in snatches, and these very troubled. Not until I received my friend's cheering news did I get a semblance of real rest.

My greatest dread was the evil that would befal the cause for which I had been fighting, and the consequences that would ensue were I taken to China and killed. Once the Chinese got me there, they would publish it abroad that I had been given up by the British Government in due legal fashion, and that there was no refuge in British territory for any of the other offenders. The members of " the Party " will remember the part played by England in the Taiping rebellion, and how by English interference that great national and Christian revolution was put down. Had I been taken to China to be executed, the people would have once more believed that the revolution was again being fought with the aid of Britain, and all hopes of success would be gone.

Had the Chinese Legation got my papers from my lodgings, further complications might have resulted to the detriment of many friends. This danger, it turned out, had been carefully guarded against by a thoughtful lady. Mrs. Cantlie, on her own responsibility, had gone to my lodgings, carefully collected my papers and correspondence, and within a few hours of her becoming acquainted with my imprisonment, there and then destroyed them. If some of my friends in various parts of the world have had no reply to their letters, they must blame this considerate lady for her wise and prompt action, and forgive my not having answered them, as I am minus their addresses, and in many cases do not even know their names. Should the Chinese authorities again entrap me, they will find no papers whereby my associates can be made known to them.

I luckily did not think of poison in my food, but my state of mind was such that food was repulsive to me. I could only get down liquid nourishment, such as milk and tea, and occasionally an egg. Only when my friend's note reached me could I either eat or sleep.

CHAPTER V

THE PART MY FRIENDS PLAYED.

OUTSIDE the Legation, I of course knew nothing of what was going on. All my appeals, all my winged scraps I had thrown out at the window, all my letters I had handed officially to Sir Halliday Macartney and Tang, I knew were useless, and worse than useless, for they but increased the closeness of my guard and rendered communication with my friends more and more an impossibility.

However, my final appeal on Friday morning, October 16th, had made an impression, for it was after that date that Cole began to interest himself in my behalf. Cole's wife had a good deal to do with the initiative, and it was Mrs. Cole who wrote a letter to Mr. Cantlie on Saturday, October 17th, 1896, and so set the machinery going. The note reached Devonshire Street at 11 p.m. Imagine the Doctor's feelings when he read the following :

" There is a friend of yours imprisoned in the Chinese Legation here since last Sunday. They intend sending him out to China, where it is certain they will hang him. It is very sad for the poor man, and unless something is done at once, he will be taken away and no one will know it. I dare not sign my name; but this is the truth, so believe what I say. Whatever you do must be done at once, or it will be too late. His name is, I believe, Lin Yin Sen."

No time was evidently to be lost. Late as it was, after ascertaining Sir Halliday Macartney's address, Mr. Cantlie set out to find him. He little knew that he was going straight to the head centre of all this disgraceful proceeding. Luckily or unluckily for me, one will never know which, he found the house, 3 Harley Place, shut up. It was 11.15 p.m. on Saturday night, and the policeman on duty in the Marylebone Road eyed him rather suspiciously as he emerged from the com pound in which the house stands. The policeman said that the house was shut up for six months, the family having gone to the country. Mr. Cantlie asked how he knew all this, and the policeman retorted that there had been a burglary attempted three nights previously, which led to close enquiries who the tenants were; therefore, the information he had, namely a six months' "anticipated" absence, was evidently definite and precise. Mr. Cantlie next drove to Marylebone Lane Police Office, and laid the matter before the Inspector on duty. He next went to Scotland Yard and asked to see the officer in charge. A Detective Inspector received him in a private room, and consented to take down his evidence. The difficulty was to get anyone to believe so improbable a story. The Police authority politely listened to the extraordinary narrative, but declared that it was impossible for Scotland Yard to take the initiative, and Mr. Cantlie found himself in the street about 1 a.m., in no better plight than when he set out.

Next morning Mr. Cantlie went to Kensington to consult with a friend as to whether or not there was any good in asking the head of the Chinese Customs in London to approach the Legation privately, and induce them to reconsider their imprudent action and ill-advised step.

Not receiving encouragement in that direction, he went again to 3 Harley Place, in hopes that at least a caretaker would be in possession, and in a position to at least tell where Sir Halliday Macartney could be found or reached by telegram. Beyond the confirmation of the policeman's story that burglary had been attempted, by seeing the evidence of "jemmies" used to break open the door, no clue could be found as to where this astute orientalised diplomatist was to be unearthed.

Mr. Cantlie then proceeded to Dr. Manson's house, and there, at his front door, he saw a man who proved to be Cole, my attendant at the Legation. The poor man had at last summoned up courage to disclose the secret of my imprisonment, and in fear and trembling sought out Mr. Cantlie at his house ; but being told he had gone to Dr. Manson's, he went on there and met both the doctors together. Cole then presented two cards I had addressed to Mr. Cantlie, stating :

"I was kidnapped on Sunday last by two Chinamen, and forcibly taken into the Chinese Legation. I am imprisoned, and in a day or two I am to be shipped off to China, on board a specially-chartered vessel. I am certain to be beheaded. Oh! woe is me."

Dr. Manson heartily joined with his friend in his attempt to rescue me, and proceeded to interrogate Cole. Mr. Cantlie remarked:

"Oh, if Sir Halliday Macartney were only in town, it would be all right. It is a pity he is away; where *can* we find him?"

Cole immediately retorted:

"Sir Halliday is in town, he comes to the Legation every day; it was Sir Halliday who locked Sun in his room, and placed me in charge, with directions to keep a strict guard over the door, that he should have no means of escape."

This information was startling, and placed the difficulty of release on a still more precarious footing. The proceedings would have to be still more carefully undertaken, and the highest authorities would have to be called in, were these crafty and masterful men to be outwitted.

Cole, in answer to further interrogations, said that it was given out in the Legation that I was a lunatic; that I was to be removed to China on the following Tuesday (that was in two days more); that he did not know by what line of ships I was going, but a man of the name of McGregor, in the City, had something to do with it. It also came out that two or three men dressed as Chinese sailors had been to the Legation during the week, and Cole had no doubt their visit had something to do with my removal, as he had never seen men of that description in the house before.

Cole left, taking a card with the names of my two friends upon it to deliver to me, in the hopes that its advent would allay my fears, and serve as a guarantee that Cole was actually working on my behalf at last. The two doctors then set out to Scotland Yard to try the effects of a further appeal in that direction. The Inspector on duty remarked : " You were here at 12.30 a.m. this morning. I am afraid it is no use your coming here again so soon." The paramount difficulty was to know where to go to represent the fact that a man's life was in danger ; that the laws of the country were being outraged ; that a man was to be practically given over, in the Metropolis of the British Empire, to be murdered.

On quitting the premises they took counsel together, and decided to invade the precincts of the Foreign Office. They were told the resident clerk would see them at five p.m. At that hour they were received, and delivered their romantic tale to the willing ears of the courteous official. Being *Sunday, of course* nothing

further could be done, but they were told
that the statement would be laid before
a higher authority on the following day.
But time was pressing, and what was to
be done ?   That night might see the
tragedy completed and the prisoner removed on board a vessel bound for
China.   What was most dreaded was
that a foreign ship would be selected;
and under a foreign flag the British
authorities were powerless.   The last
hope was that, if I were removed before
they succeeded in rousing the authorities
and the vessel actually got away, that it
might be stopped and searched in the
Suez Canal; but, were I shipped on
board a vessel under a flag other than
British, this hope would prove a delusion.
With this dread upon them, they decided
to take the decisive step of going to the
Legation, and telling the Chinese that
they were acquainted with the fact that
Sun was a prisoner in their hands, and

that the British Government and the police knew of their intention to remove him to China for execution. Dr. Manson decided he should go alone, as Mr Cantlie's name in connection with Sun's was well known at the Legation.

Accordingly Dr. Manson called alone at 49 Portland Place. The powdered footman at the door was asked to call one of the English-speaking Chinamen. Presently the Chinese interpreter, my captor and tormentor, Tang himself, appeared. Dr. Manson said he wanted to see Sun Yat Sen. A puzzled expression fell o'er Tang's face, as though seeking to recall such a name. " Sun !—Sun ! there is no such person here." Dr. Manson then proceeded to inform him that he was quite well aware that Sun was here; that he wished to inform the Legation that the Foreign Office had been made cognisant of the fact : and that Scotland Yard was posted in the

matter of Sun's detention.   But a Chinese
diplomatist is nothing if not a capable
liar, and Tang's opportunity of lying
must have satisfied even his Oriental
liking for the *rôle*.   With the semblance
of truth in his every word and action,
Tang assured his interrogator that the
whole thing was nonsense, and that no
such person was there.   His openness
and frankness partly shook Dr. Manson's
belief in my condition, and when he got
back to Mr. Cantlie's he was so impressed
with the apparent truthfulness of. Tang s
statement, that he even suggested that
the tale of my imprisonment might be a
trick by myself to some end—he knew
not what.   Thus can my countrymen lie ;
Tang even shook the belief of a man
like Dr. Manson, who had lived in China
twenty-two years ; who spoke the Amoy
dialect fluently ; and was thereby more
intimately acquainted with the Chinese
and their ways than nine-tenths of the

people who visit the Far East. However, he had to dismiss the thought, as no ulterior object could be seen in a trick of the kind. Tang is sure to rise high in the service of his country ; a liar like that is sure to get his reward amongst a governing class who exist and thrive upon it.

It was seven o'clock on Sunday evening when the two doctors desisted from their labours, parted company, and considered they had done their duty. But they were still not satisfied that I was safe. The danger was that I might be removed that very night, especially since the Legation knew the British Government were now aware of the fact, and that if immediate embarkation were not possible, a change of residence of their victim might be contemplated. This was a very probable step indeed, and, if it had been possible, there is no doubt it would have been accomplished. Luckily for me, the Marquis Tseng, as he is called, had shortly before left London for China, and given up his residence. Had it not been so, it is quite possible the plan of removal to his house would have recommended itself to my clever countryman ; and when it was accomplished, they would have thrown themselves upon the confidence and good friendship of the British, and asked them to search the house That ruse could not be carried out ; but the removal to the docks was quite feasible. It was expected I was to sail on Tuesday, and, as the ship must be now in dock, there was nothing more likely than that the " lunatic " passenger should be taken on board at night, to escape the excitement and noise of the daily traffic in the streets.

CHAPTER VI.

THE SEARCH FOR A DETECTIVE.

WITH all this in his mind Mr. Cantlie set forth again, this time to search out some means of having the Legation watched. He called at a friend's house and obtained the address of Slater's firm of private detectives in the City. Hither he went; but Slater's office was closed.

On Sunday it would seem no detectives are required. Can no trouble arise on Sunday in England? It must be remembered that the division of the month is but an artificial and mundane convenience, and crime does not always accommodate itself to such vagaries of the calendar as the portioning the month into weeks. However, there was the hard fact, Slater's

office was shut, and neither shouting, bell-
ringing, nor hard knocks could elicit any
response from the granite buildings in
Basinghall Street.

A consultation in the street with a
policeman and the friendly cabman, who
was taken into the secret of my detention,
ended in a call at the nearest police sta-
tion. Here the tale had to be unfolded
again, and all the doubts as to the doctor's
soberness and sanity set at rest before
anything further could be attempted.

"Where was the place?"

"Portland Place, West."

"Oh! it is no good coming here, you
must go back to the West End; we belong
to the City police."

To the doctor's mind neither eastern
nor western police were of any avail.

"However," he persisted, "could a
detective not be obtained to watch the
house?"

"No. It was out of the power of the

City police to interfere in the West End work."

" Have you not some old police constable, a reserve man, who would be willing to earn a little money at a job of the kind?" Mr. Cantlie asked.

" Well, there might be—let us see."

And here a number of men fell good-naturedly to discussing whom they could recall to memory. Well, yes; they thought So-and-so would do.

" Where does he live?"

"Oh! he lives in Leytonstone. You could not get him to-night: this is Sunday, you know."

Sunday I should think it was, and my head in the balance. After a long discussion a man's name was suggested, and they got rid of the persistent doctor. The man's address was Gibston Square, Islington.

But before starting thence, Mr. Cantlie thought he would give the newspapers the whole tale, so he drove to the *Times* Office and asked for the sub-editor. A card to fill in was handed him as to the nature of his business; and he wrote:

"Case of Kidnapping at the Chinese Legation!"

This was 9 p.m., and he was told no one would be in until 10 p.m.

Away then he went to Islington in search of his "man." After a time the darkly-lit square was found, and the number proving correct, the abode was entered. But again disappointment followed; for "he could not go, but he thought he knew a man that would." Well, there was no help for it; but where did this man live? He was a wonderful chap; but the card bearing his address could not be found. High and low was it looked for: drawers and boxes, old packets of letters and unused waistcoats were searched and turned out. At last, however, it was unearthed, and then it was known that the man was not at home, but was watching a public-house in the City.

Well, even this was overcome, for the Doctor suggested that one of the numerous children that crowded the parlour should be sent with a note to the home address of the detective, whilst the father of the flock should accompany the Doctor to the City in search of the watcher. At last the hansom cab drew up at a little distance from a public-house, somewhere in the neighbourhood of the Barbican, and the place was reconnoitred But no watcher could be seen around, and a futile search was settled in this way : that the public-house should be watched until eleven o'clock, when the house closed, at which time in all probability the " man " would be forthcoming. Mr. Cantlie left his erstwhile friend outside the house and set off again for the *Times* Office. There he was received in " audience " and his statement was taken down, and the publication of the tale was left to the *Times'* discretion.   By this time it was 11.30 p.m. on Sunday, and at last the restless Doctor sought his home.   He was somewhat chagrined to find that at 12 midnight his expected detective had not yet appeared, but, nothing daunted, he prepared to keep watch himself.   He said good-night to his wife, and set out to observe the Legation, ready to interfere actively if need be.

However, as he strode forth with valiant intent, the Doctor encountered his expected "man" in the street, and immediately posted him.   His Gibston Square friend had proved himself reliable and sent his deputy.   The windows of the Legation, late as it was,—past twelve at night,—were still lit up, indicating a commotion within, the result, no doubt, of Dr. Manson's intimation that their evil ways were no longer unknown.   The "man" was placed in a hansom cab in

Weymouth Street, under the shadow of a house on the south side of the street, between Portland Place and Portland Road. It was a beautiful moonlight night, and both the Legation entrances could be clearly seen. The hansom cab was a necessary part of the sentinel on duty, as, supposing I had been hurried from the house across the pavement and into a carriage, I should have been carried beyond the reach of a person on foot in a few minutes. Cabs cannot be had at any moment in the early morning hours; hence the necessary precaution of having the watchman in a position by which he could follow in pursuit, if he were required so to do. The newspapers had it, that the cab was intended to carry me off when the rescue party had freed me, but this is another part of the story which I will relate later on.

At 2 a.m. the Doctor got to bed, and having informed the Government, told

the police, given the tale to the newspapers, posted private detectives for the
night, his day's work was finished and
practically my life was saved, although I
did not know it.

———

CHAPTER VII.

THE GOVERNMENT INTERVENE.

ON Monday, October 19th, Slater's office was again asked for detectives, and, when they came, they were posted with instructions to watch the Legation night and day.

At 12 noon, by appointment at the Foreign Office, Mr. Cantlie submitted his statement in writing. The Foreign Office were evidently anxious that some less official plan of release should be effected than by their active interference, in the hopes that international complications might be averted.

Moreover, the proofs of my detention were mere hearsay, and it was unwise to raise a question which seemed to be

founded on an improbable statement.
As a step in the evidence, enquiry was
made at the "Glen" Line Office, and
when it was found that a passage had
been asked for, the Government then
knew by direct evidence that the tale was
not only true, but that actual steps for
its execution had been carefully laid.
From this moment the affair passed into
Government hands, and my friends were
relieved of their responsibility.

Six detectives were told off by Government for duty outside the Legation, and
the police in the neighbourhood were
made cognisant of the facts and apprised
to be vigilant.

The police had, moreover, my photograph, which I had had taken in America
in my European dress. To the eye of the
foreigner, who has not travelled in China,
all Chinese are alike, so that an ordinary
photograph was not likely to be of much
assistance; but in this photograph I wore

a moustache and had my hair " European fashion."

No Chinaman wears a moustache until he has attained the "rank" of grand-father; but even in the country of early marriages, I, who have not yet attained the age of thirty, can scarcely aspire to the "distinction."

On Thursday, October 22nd, a writ of *Habeas Corpus* was made out against either the Legation or Sir Halliday Macartney, I know not which, but the Judge at the Old Bailey would not agree to the action, and it fell through.

On the afternoon of the same day a special correspondent of the *Globe* called at Mr. Cantlie's house and asked him if he knew anything about a Chinaman that had been kidnapped by the Chinese Legation. Well, he thought he did; what did the *Globe* know about it ? The Doctor said he had given the information to the *Times* on Sunday, October 18th,

five days before, and further supple-
mented it by additional information on
Monday, October 19th, and that he felt
bound to let the *Times* make it public
first.   However, Mr. Cantlie said, " Read
over what you have written about the
circumstance, and I will tell you if it is
correct."   The information the *Globe* had
received proving correct, the Doctor en-
dorsed it, but requested his name not to
be mentioned.

Of course many persons were acquainted
with the circumstances long before they
appeared in print.   Some two or three
hundred people knew of my imprisonment
by Tuesday morning, and it was a wonder
that the ever eager correspondents did
not know of it before Thursday afternoon.
However, once it got wind there was no
hushing the matter up, for from the
moment the *Globe* published the startling
news, there was no more peace at 46
Devonshire Street, W.

Within two hours after the issue of the fifth edition of the *Globe*, Mr. Cantlie was interviewed by a Central News and a *Daily Mail* reporter. He was too reticent to please them, but the main outlines were extracted from him.

The two searchers after truth next called at the Chinese Legation and asked to see Sun. They were met by the ever-ready and omnipresent Tang, who denied all knowledge of such a man. Tang was shown the report in the *Globe*, at which he laughed merrily and said the whole thing was a huge imposition. The Central News reporter, however, said it was no good denying it, and that if Sun was not given up, he might expect 10,000 men here to-morrow to pull the place about his ears. Nothing, however, moved Tang, and he lied harder than ever.

Sir Halliday Macartney was next un-earthed at the Midland Hotel and interviewed. His statements are best gathered from the Press reports.

Sir Halliday Macartney, Counsellor of the Chinese Legation, visited the Foreign Office at 3.30 yesterday afternoon. In conversation with a press representative, Sir Halliday said: I am unable to give you any information about the man detained at the Legation, beyond what has already appeared in print. On being informed that the Foreign Office had just issued an announcement to the effect that Lord Salisbury had requested the Chinese Minister to release the prisoner, Sir Halliday admitted that this was so, and in answer to a further question as to what would be the result of the request, replied: "The man will be released, but this will be done strictly without prejudice to the rights of the Legation involved."

In course of a later conversation with a representative of the press, Sir Halliday Macartney said: Sun Yat Sen is not the name of the man whom we have in detention upstairs. We have no doubt of his real identity, and have been from time to time fully informed of all his movements since he set foot in England. He came of his own free will to the Legation, and was certainly not kidnapped or forced or inveigled into the premises. It is quite a usual thing for solitary Chinamen in London to call here to make casual inquiries, or to have a chat with a countryman. There appears, moreover, to be some ground for suspecting that this peculiar visitor, believing himself unknown, came with some idea of spying on us and getting some information. Nobody knew him by sight. When he called he got into conversation with one of our staff, and was afterwards introduced to me. We chatted for awhile, and some remarks he made led me after he had gone to suspect he might be the person we were having watched. These suspicions being confirmed, he was, on returning the following day, detained, and he is still under detention pending instructions from the Chinese Government.

Speaking on the international side of the matter, Sir Halliday said: The man is not a British, but a Chinese, subject. We contend that for certain purposes the Legation is Chinese territory, where the Chinese Minister alone has jurisdiction. If a Chinaman comes here voluntarily, and if there are charges or suspicions against him, we contend that no one outside has any right to interfere with his detention. It would be quite different if he were outside this building, for then he would be on British territory, and we could not arrest him without a warrant.

Answering further questions, Sir Halliday mentioned that the man was not treated like a prisoner, and every consideration had been paid to his comfort. Sir Halliday ridiculed the statement which has appeared that the captive might be subjected to torture or undue pressure.　He added a statement that a letter of inquiry had been received from the Foreign Office on the subject, which would receive immediate attention.

The Central News says: Sir Halliday Macartney, on his return to the Chinese Legation from the Foreign Office, proceeded to the bedside of the Minister Kung Ta Jen, and explained to him that Lord Salisbury had insisted upon the release of Sun Yat Sen.

It is not for me to discuss the behaviour of Sir Halliday Macartney; I leave that to public opinion and to his own conscience. In his own mind, I have no doubt, he has reasons for his action; but they seem scarcely consistent with those of a sane man, let alone the importance of the position he occupies. I expect Tang expressed the position pretty exactly when he told me that " the Minister is but a figure-head here, Macartney is the ruler."

Various reports of an intended rescue crept into the newspapers. The following is an example:

AN INTENDED RESCUE.

In reference to the arrest of Sun Yat Sen, it has been ascertained that his friends had arranged a bold scheme to bring about his rescue. Had they not been definitely assured by the Foreign Office and Scotland Yard that no harm whatever should come to him, his rescue was to be effected by means of breaking the window of his room, and descending from the roof of No. 51 Portland Place, the residence of Viscount Powerscourt. His friends had succeeded in informing him of the plan they intended to pursue, and although information which was subsequently obtained pointed to the fact that Sun Yat Sen was being kept handcuffed, a promise of inside assistance in opening the window satisfied his friends of the feasibility of the plan. Indeed, so far matured was the scheme, that a cab was held in waiting to convey Sun Yat Sen to the home of a friend. By the prisoner's friends it is declared that Long, the interpreter at the Legation, was one of the Chinamen who actually decoyed Sun into the Legation, though he was invariably the most positive subsequently in denying that such a man had ever been inside the Legation walls. His friends declare that Sun was dressed in English clothes, and so far from his being a typical Oriental, when dressed according to Western fashion was invariably taken for an Englishman. He is declared to be a man of unbounded good nature and of the gentlest dispo-

sition in Hongkong, and the various places where
he practised medicine he obtained a reputation for
skill and benevolence towards the poor. He is
believed to have been in a great extent the tool
of the Canton conspirators, though he never
hesitated to condemn the cruel and oppressive
Government of the Viceroy of Canton. He is
said to have journeyed throughout Canton in
the interests of his society, and the plot itself
is declared to be the most widespread and formidable since the present Emperor commenced
to reign.

The real facts are these.   Cole sent the
following communication to Mr. Cantlie
on October 19th, 1896: "I shall have a
good opportunity to let Mr. Sun out on to
the roof of the next house in Portland
Place to-night.   If you think it advisable,
get permission from the occupants of the
house to have someone waiting there to
receive him.   If I am to do it, find means
to let me know."   Mr. Cantlie went with
this letter to Scotland Yard and requested
that a constable be posted with himself on
the roof of the house in question ; but the

Scotland Yard authorities, thinking it was an undignified proceeding, dissuaded him from his purpose, and gave it as their firm conviction that I should walk out by the front door in a day or two.

CHAPTER VIII.

RELEASED.

ON October 22nd Cole directed my attention to the coal scuttle, and when he left the room I picked up a clipping from a newspaper, which proved to be the *Globe*. There I read the account of my detention, under the heading: "*Startling Story! Conspirator Kidnapped in London! Imprisonment at the Chinese Embassy!*" And then followed a long and detailed account of my position. At last the Press had interfered, and I felt that I was really safe. It came as a reprieve to a condemned man, and my heart was full of thankfulness.

Friday, October 23rd, dawned, and the day wore on, and still I was in durance.

At 4.30 p.m., however, on that day, my English and Chinese guards came into the room and said "Macartney wants to see you downstairs." I was told to put on my boots and hat and overcoat. I accordingly did so, not knowing whither I was going. I descended the stairs, and as it was to the basement I was being conducted, I believed I was to be hidden in a cellar whilst the house was being searched by the command of the British Government. I was not told I was to be released, and I thought I was to enter another place of imprisonment or punishment. It seemed too good to be true that I was actually to be released. However, Mr. Cantlie presently appeared on the scene in company with two other men, who turned out to be Inspector Jarvis from Scotland Yard, and an old man, the messenger from the Foreign Office.

Sir Halliday Macartney then, in the presence of these gentlemen, handed me over the various effects that had been taken from me, and addressed the Government officials to the following effect :—

" I hand this man over to you, and I do so on condition that neither the prerogative nor the diplomatic rights of the Legation are interfered with," or words to that effect. I was too excited to commit them to memory, but they seemed to me then, as they do now, senseless and childish.

The meeting related above took place in a passage in the basement of the house, and I was told I was a free man. Sir Halliday then shook hands with us all, a post-Judas salutation, and we were shown out by a side-door leading to the area. From thence we ascended the area steps, and issued into Weymouth Street from the back door of the Legation.

It will perhaps escape observation and pass out of mind as but a minor circumstance that we were sent out by the *back* door of the Legation.

The fact of the rescue was the all important measure in the minds of the little group of Englishmen present; not so, however, with my astute countryman; not so especially with Sir Halliday Macartney, that embodiment of retrograde orientalism.

The fact that the representatives of the British Government were shown out by the back door, as common carrion, will redound to the credit of the Minister and his *clientelle* in the high courts of their country. It was intended as a slight and insult, and it was carried out as only one versed in the Chinese methods of dealing with foreigners can appreciate. The excuse, no doubt, was that the hall was crowded with reporters; that a considerable throng of people had assembled in the street outside the building; that the Foreign Office was anxious that the affair should be conducted quietly without demonstration. These, no doubt, were the reasons present in the ever-ready minds of these Manchurian rapscallions and their caretaker Macartney.

To English ways of looking at things, the fact of my release was all that was cared for; but to the Chinese the manner of the release wiped out all the triumph of British diplomacy in obtaining it. Both had their triumph, and no doubt it brought them equal gratification.

It was not an imposing party that proceeded to the Chinese Legation that Friday afternoon in October; but one member of it, the venerable old messenger from the Foreign Office, had a small note concealed in the depths of his great-coat pocket that seemed to bear great weight. It must have been short and to the point, for it took Macartney but two or three seconds to master its contents. Short it may have been, but it bore the sweet message of freedom for me, and an escape from death, and what I dreaded more, the customary exquisite torture to which political prisoners in China are submitted to procure confession of the names of accomplices.

In Weymouth Street a considerable crowd had assembled, and the ever-present newspaper reporter tried to inveigle me there and then into a confession. I was, however, speedily put into a four-wheeled cab, and, in company with Mr. Cantlie, Inspector Jarvis, and the messenger, driven off towards Scotland Yard. On the way thither Inspector Jarvis gravely lectured me on my delinquencies, and scolded me as a bad boy, and advised me to have nothing to do any more with revolutions. Instead of stopping at Scotland Yard, however, the cab drew up at the door of a restaurant in Whitehall, and we got out on the pavement. Immediately the newspaper men surrounded

me; where they came from I could not
tell. We had left them a mile away in
Portland Place, and here they were again
the moment my cab stopped. There is
no repressing them; one man had actually, unknown to us, climbed up on the
seat beside the driver. He it was that
stayed the cab at the restaurant, knowing
well that if once I was within the precincts
of Scotland Yard they could not get at
me for some time. Unless the others—
some dozen in number—were on the roof
of my cab, I cannot understand where
they sprang from. I was hustled from
the pavement into the back premises of
the hostelry with much more violence than
ever was expended upon me when origin-
ally taken within the Chinese Legation,
and surrounded by a crowd thirsting for
knowledge as eagerly as my countrymen
thirsted for my head. Pencils executed
wonderful hieroglyphics which I had never
seen before, and I did not know until that

moment that English could be written in what seemed to me cuneiform characters. I found out afterwards it was in shorthand they were writing.

I spoke until I could speak no more, and it was only when Mr. Cantlie called out "Time, gentlemen!" that I was forcibly rescued from their midst and carried off to Scotland Yard. At the Yard I was evidently regarded as a child of their own delivery, and Jarvis's honest face was a picture to behold. However, the difficult labour was over, and here I was free to make my own confession. I was detained there for an hour, during which time I made a full statement of the circumstances of my capture and detention. This was all taken down and read over to me, and I appended my signature and bade a cordial adieu to my friends in the police force Mr. Cantlie and myself then hied ourselves homewards, where a hospitable welcome was accorded me, and

over an appetising dinner, a toast to my
"head" was drunk with enthusiasm.

During the evening I was frequently
interviewed, and it was not until a late
hour that I was allowed to rest. Oh!
that first night's sleep! Shall I ever
forget it? For nine hours did it last, and
when I awoke it was to the noise of
children romping on the floor above me.
It was evident by their loud, penetrating
voices some excitement was on hand, and
as I listened I could hear the cause of it.
"Now, Colin, you be Sun Yat Sen, and
Neil will be Sir Halliday Macartney,
and I will rescue Sun." Then followed a
turmoil; Sir Halliday was knocked end-
ways, and a crash on the floor made me
believe that my little friend Neil was no
more. Sun was brought out in triumph
by Keith, the eldest boy, and a general
amnesty was declared by the beating of
drums, the piercing notes of a tin whistle,
and the singing of " The British Grena-

diers." This was home and safety, indeed; for it was evident my youthful friends were prepared to shed the last drop of their blood on my behalf.

During Saturday, October 24th, I was interviewing all day. The one question put was, " How did you let the doctors know ? " and the same question was addressed to Mr. Cantlie many scores of times. We felt, however, that our tongues were tied; as, by answering the query, we should be incriminating those who, within the Legation walls, had acted as my friends, and they would lose their positions. However, when Cole resolved to resign his appointment, so that none of the others should be wrongly suspected, there was no object in hiding who had been the informant. It is all very well to say that I bribed him; that is not the case. He did not understand that I gave him the money by way of fee at all; he believed I gave it him to keep for me; he told Mr.

Cantlie he had the £20 the day he got it, and offered to give it to him for safe keeping. When I came out Cole handed the money back to me, but it was the least I could do to urge him to keep it. I wish it had been more, but it was all the ready money I had. Cole had many frights during this time, but perhaps the worst scare he got was at the very first start. On the Sunday afternoon, October 18th, when he had made up his mind to help me practically, he took my notes to Mr. Cantlie, in his pocket, at 46 Devonshire Street. The door was opened and he was admitted within the hall. The doctor was not at home, so he asked to see his wife. Whilst the servant was gone to fetch her mistress, Cole became conscious of the presence of a Chinaman watching him from the far end of the hall. He immediately suspected that he had been followed or rather anticipated, for here was a Chinaman, pigtail and all, earnestly scrutinising him from a recess. When Mrs. Cantlie came down she beheld a man, trembling with fear and pale from terror, who could hardly speak. The cause of this alarm was a model of a Chinaman, of most life-like appearance, which Mr. Cantlie had brought home with him amongst his curios from Hong Kong. It has frightened many other visitors with less tender consciences than Cole's, whose overwrought nerves actually endowed the figure with a halo of terrible reality. Mrs. Cantlie relieved Cole's mind from his fear and sent him in to find her husband at Dr. Manson's. My part of the tale is nearly ended; what further complications in connection with this affair may arise I cannot say. There is not time, as yet, to hear how the papers in other English-speaking countries will deal with the subject, and as Parliament has not yet assembled I cannot say what questions appertaining to the event may be forthcoming. I have, however, found many friends since my release. I have paid several pleasant visits to the country. I have been dined and feasted, and run a good chance of being permanently spoiled by my well-wishers in and around London.

Appendix.

I APPEND a few of the numerous articles called forth by my arrest. The first is a letter from Professor Holland to *The Times*, and is headed ·

THE CASE OF SUN YAT SEN.

To the Editor of THE TIMES.

Sir,—The questions raised by the imprisonment of Sun Yat Sen are two in number. First, was the act of the Chinese Minister in detaining him an unlawful act? And secondly, if so, what steps could properly have been taken to obtain his release had it been refused?

The reply to the former question is not far to seek. The claim of an Ambassador to exercise any sort of domestic jurisdiction, even over members of his suite, is now little heard of, although, in 1603, Sully, when French Ambassador, went so far as to sentence one of his *attachés* to death, handing him over to the Lord Mayor for execution. I can recall but one instance of an attempt on the part of a Minister to exercise constraint against a person unconnected with his mission. In 1642, Leitao, Portuguese Minister at the Hague, detained in his house a horse-dealer who had cheated him. The result was a riot, in which the hotel was plundered, and Wicquefort remarks upon the transaction that Leitao, who had given public lectures on the Law of Nations, ought to have known *qu'il ne lui estoit pas permis de faire une prison de sa maison.* Sun Yat Sen, while on British soil as a *subditus temporarius,* was under the protection of our Laws, and his confinement in the Chinese Legation was a high offence against the rights of the British Crown.

The second question, though not so simple, presents no serious difficulty. A refusal on the part of the Chinese Minister to release his prisoner would have been a sufficient ground for requesting him to leave the country. If this mode of proceeding would have been too dilatory for the exigencies of the case, it can hardly be doubted that the circumstances would have justified an entry upon the Legation premises by the London police. An Ambassador's hotel is said to be "extra-territorial," but this too compendious phrase means no more than that the hotel is for certain purposes inaccessible to the ordinary jurisdiction of the country in which it stands. The exemptions thus enjoyed are, however, strictly defined by usage, and new exemptions cannot be deduced from a metaphor. The case of Gyllenburg, in 1717, showed that if a Minister is suspected of conspiring against the Government to which he is accredited he may be arrested and his cabinets may be ransacked. The case of the coachman of Mr. Gallatin, in 1827, establishes that, after courteous notice, the police may enter a Legation in order to take into custody one of its servants who has been guilty of an offence elsewhere. There is also a general agreement that, except possibly in Spain and in the South American Republics, the hotel is no longer an asylum for even political offenders. Still less can it be supposed that an illegal imprisonment in a Minister's residence will not be put an end to by such action of the local police as may be necessary.

It seems needless to inquire into the responsibility which would rest upon the Chinese authorities if Sun Yat Sen was, as he alleges, kidnapped in the open street, or would have rested upon them had they removed him through the streets, with a view to shipping him off to China. Acts of this kind find no defenders. What is admitted to have occurred is sufficiently serious, and was doubtless due to excess of zeal on the part of the subordinates of the Chinese Legation. International law has long been ably taught by Dr. Martin at the Tung-wen College of Peking, and the Imperial Government cannot be supposed to be indifferent to a strict conformity to the precepts of the science on the part of its representatives at foreign Courts.

I am, Sir, your obedient servant,

T. E. HOLLAND.

OXFORD, *October 24th.*

Another legal opinion is referred to below :

LEGAL OPINION.

Mr. Cavendish, one of the best authorities on the law of extradition, informed an interviewer at Bow Street yesterday that, speaking from memory, he could cite no case at all parallel with the case of Sun Yat Sen. The case of the Zanzibar Pretender was, of course, in no way parallel, for he took refuge in the German Consulate. He threw himself on the hospitality of the German Government, which, following the procedure sanctioned by International Law, refuses to give him up, and conveyed him to German territory on the mainland. Sun Yat Sen's case was that of an alleged Chinese subject, having come within the walls of the Legation of his own country, was arrested by representatives of his own Government for an offence against that Government. Mr. Cavendish assumed that if the facts were as stated, the case could only be dealt with by diplomatic representation on the part of our Foreign Office, and not by any known legal rule.

The next is a letter from Mr. James G. Wood to the same paper discussing some of the points of law raised in Professor Holland's letter:

To the Editor of THE TIMES.

Sir,—The second question proposed by Professor Holland, though fortunately, under the circumstances, not of present importance, is deserving of careful consideration. I venture to think his answer to it unsatisfactory.

It is suggested that on a refusal by the Chinese Minister to release his prisoner, "it can hardly be doubted that the circumstances would have justified an entry on the Legation premises by the London police." But why there should not be such a doubt is not explained. This is not solving the question but guessing at its solution. The London police have no roving commission to release persons unlawfully detained in London houses; and anyone attempting to enter for such a purpose could be lawfully resisted by force.

The only process known to the law as applicable to a case of unlawful detention is a writ of *habeas corpus*, and this is where the real difficulty lies. Could such a writ be addressed to an Ambassador or any member of the Legation? Or if it were, and it were disregarded, could process of contempt follow? I venture to think not; and I know of no precedent for such proceeding.

I agree that the phrase that an Ambassador's hotel is extra-territorial is so metaphysical as to be misleading. It is, in fact, inaccurate. The more careful writers do not use it. The true proposition is not that the residence is extra-territorial in the sense in which a ship is often said to be so, but the Minister himself is deemed to be so; and as a consequence he and the members of his family and suite are said to enjoy a complete immunity from all civil process. It is not a question of what may or may not be done in the residence, but what may or may not be done to individuals. That being so, the process I have mentioned appears to involve a breach of the comity of nations.

To adduce cases where the police have under a warrant entered an Embassy to arrest persons who have committed an offence elsewhere to found the proposition that "the local police may take action to put an end to an illegal imprisonment," begun and continued within the Embassy, does not land us on safe ground. There is no common feature in the two cases.

I am, Sir, your obedient servant,

JAMES G. WOOD.

October 27th.

THE SUPPOSED CHINESE REVOLUTIONIST.

[*From the* CHINA MAIL, *Hong Kong, Dec. 3rd, 1896.*]

Sun Yat Sen, who has recently been in trouble in London through the Chinese Minister attempting to kidnap him for execution as a rebel, is not unlikely to become a prominent character in history. Of course, it would not be right to state, until a duly constituted court of law has found, that a man is definitely connected with any illegal movement, or that any movement with which he is connected is definitely anti-dynastic. The only suggestion of Dr. Sun Yat Sen being a rebel in any sense comes from the Chinese Legation in London and the officials of Canton. But without any injury to him it may be safely said that he is a remarkable man, with most enlightened views on the undoubtedly miserable state of China's millions, and that there are many Chinese who feel very strongly on the subject and try now and then to act very strongly. The allegation of the officials is that these people tried to accomplish a revolution in October, 1895, and that Sun Yat Sen was a leader in the conspiracy. Foreigners, even those resident in the Far East, had little knowledge how near the long-expected break-up of China then was. As it happened, the outbreak missed fire, and what little attention it did attract was of the contemptuous sort. The situation was, however, one of as great danger as any since the Tai Pings were suppressed, and the organisation was much more up-to-date and on a more enlightened basis than even that great rebellion. In fact, it was the intelligence of the principal movers that caused the movement to be discountenanced at an early stage as premature, instead of struggling on with a more disastrous failure in view, for the revolution is only postponed, not abandoned for ever. The origin of the movement cannot be specifically traced; it arose from the general dis-satisfaction of Chinese with Manchu rule, and it came to a head on the outbreak of war between China and Japan. The malcontents saw that the war afforded an opportunity to put their aspirations into shape, and they promptly set to work. At first, that is to say before China had been so soundly thrashed all along the line, they had in view purely lawful and constitutional measures, and hoped to effect radical changes without resort to violence. Dr. Sun worked hard and loyally to fuse the inchoate elements of disaffection brought into existence by Manchu misgovernment, and to give the whole reform movement a purely constitutional form, in the earnest hope of raising his wretched country out of the Slough of Despond in which it was and is sinking deeper daily. His was the master-mind that strove to subdue the wild uncontrollable spirits always prominent in Chinese reactionary schemes, to harmonise conflicting interests, not only as between various parties in his own country but also as between Chinese and foreigners, and as between various foreign Powers. The most difficult problem was to work out the sequel of any upheaval—to anticipate and be ready in advance to deal with all the complications bound to ensue as soon as the change took place. Moreover he had to bear in mind that any great reform movement must necessarily depend very largely on the aid of foreigners, of nations and individuals as well, while there is throughout China an immense mass of anti-foreign prejudice which would have to be overcome somehow. The task was stupendous, hopeless in fact, but he recognised that the salvation of China depended and still depends on something of the sort being some day rendered possible, and that the only way to accomplish it was to try, try, try again. That is to say, last year's attempt was not likely to succeed, but was likely to bring success a stage nearer, and in that sense it was well worth the effort to an ardent patriot. Dr. Sun was the only man who combined a complete grasp of the situation with a reckless bravery of the kind which alone can make a national regeneration. He was born in Honolulu, and had a good English education. He has travelled extensively in Europe and America, and is a young man of remarkable attainments. He was for some time a medical student in Dr. Kerr's School in Tientsin, and afterwards was on the staff of the Alice Memorial Hospital in Hong Kong. He is of average height, thin and wiry, with a keenness of expression and frankness of feature seldom seen in Chinese. An unassuming manner and an earnestness of speech, combined with a quick perception and resolute judgment, go to impress one with the conviction that he is in every way an exceptional type of his race. Beneath his calm exterior is hidden a personality that cannot but be a great influence for good in China sooner or later, if the Fates are fair. In China, any advocate of reform or any foe of corruption and oppression is liable to be regarded as a violent revolutionist, and summarily executed. It has been the same in the history of every country when freedom and enlightenment were in their infancy, or not yet born. The propaganda had therefore to be disseminated with the greatest care, and at imminent peril. First, an able and exhaustive treatise on political matters was published in Hong Kong, and circulated all over China, especially in the south, where it created a sensation, early in 1895. It was most cautiously worded, and the most censorious official could not lay his finger on a word of it and complain; but it depicted in vivid colours the beauties of enlightened and honest government, contrasted with the horrors of corrupt and tyrannical misgovernment. This feeler served to show how much voluntary reform could be expected of Chinese officialdom, for it had as much effect as a volume of sermons thrown among a shoal of sharks. Then it became no longer possible to control the spirits of insurrection. Steps were at once taken to organise a rebellion, with which it is alleged, but not yet proved, that Dr. Sun Yat Sen was associated. Before the war there had been insurrectionary conspiracies—in fact, such things are chronic in China. The navy was disaffected, because of certain gross injustices and extortions practised on the officers and men by the all-powerful mandarins. The commanders of land forces and forts were not much different, and many civilian officials were willing to join in a rising. No doubt much of the support accorded to the scheme was prompted by ulterior motives, for there are more of that sort than of any other in China. The rebellion was almost precipitated in March, when funds were supplied from Honolulu, Singapore, Australia, and elsewhere; but men of the right sort were still wanting, and arms had not been obtained in great quantity, and wiser counsels prevailed. It would have been better perhaps if wiser counsels had prevailed in October, but wisdom cannot come without experience, and for the sake of the experience the leaders of the abortive revolution do not greatly regret their action. Some indeed drew out as soon as it became certain that violent measures were to be adopted; but the penalty of death would not be obviated by that, and it was at imminent risk of his life that Dr. Sun had been travelling throughout the length and breadth of China, preaching the gospel of good government and gathering recruits for constitutional reform.

His allies, never very confident in pacific methods, planned a bold *coup d'état*, which might have gained a momentary success, but made no provision for what would happen in the next few moments. Men were drafted to Hong Kong to be prepared for an attack on Canton; arms and ammunition were smuggled in cement-casks; money was subscribed lavishly, foreign advisers and commanders were obtained, and attempts were made, without tangible result, to secure the co-operation of the Japanese Government. What would have been the result if the verbal sympathy of Japanese under-officials had been followed by active sympathy in higher quarters, none can tell; the indemnity, the Liao-tung settlement, the commercial treaty, the whole history of the relations between Japan and China and Europe since the war might have been totally different. Every detail of the plot was arranged, but before the time for striking the blow, treachery stepped in. A prominent Chinese merchant of Hong Kong had professed adherence to the reform movement, for he had much to gain by it; then he concluded that he could gain more by playing into the hands of the official vampires, for he was connected with one of the many syndicates formed to compete for railway and mining concessions in China after the war. So he gave information, and the cement was examined, with the result that the whole *coup d'état* was nothing more than a flash in the pan. Dr. Sun happened to be in Canton at the time, and was accused of active participation in the violent section of the reform movement. In China, to be innocent is not to be safe; an accusation is none the less dangerous for being utterly unfounded. Sun had to fly for his life, without a moment's deliberation as to friends or property or anything else; and for two or three weeks he was a fugitive hiding in the labyrinthine canals and impenetrable pirate-haunts of the great Kwang-tung Delta. A report has been published that forty or fifty of his supposed accomplices were executed, and a reward was offered for his arrest, but he got away to Honolulu and thence to America. The story goes that this indomitable patriot immediately set to work converting the Chinese at the Washington Embassy to the cause of reform, and that afterwards he tried to do the same in London; that one of the Chinese in the Legation at Washington had professed sympathy with the apostle of enlightenment, and then thought more money could be made on the other side, and so telegraphed to the London Embassy to arrest Sun and kidnap him back to China by hook or by crook. However that may be, he was captured and confined in a most outrageous manner in the London Legation, whatever plausible piffle may be put forward by Sir Halliday Macartney, or any servile prevaricator; and it is due to Dr. Cantlie, Sun's friend and teacher in Hong Kong, that one of the best men China has ever produced was rescued by British justice from the toils of treacherous mandarindom. All who know Dr. Cantlie—and he is well known in many parts of the world—agree that a more upright, honourable and devoted bene- factor of humanity has never breathed. Dr. Sun is in good hands, and under the protection of such a man as Dr. Cantlie there can be little doubt that he will pursue his chosen career with single- hearted enthusiasm and most scrupulous straight- forwardness of methods, until at last the good work of humanising the miserable condition of the Chinese Empire is brought to a satisfactory state of perfection.

A leading article in *The Times* of Saturday, October 24th, 1896, discusses the question very fully:

While the " Concert of Europe " is supposed to be making steady progress towards the establish- ment of harmony amongst the constituent Powers, the ordinarily smooth course of diplomatic inter- course has been ruffled by a curious violation of law and custom at the Chinese Legation—a violation which might have led to tragic con- sequences, but which has so turned out as to present chiefly a ludicrous side for our con- sideration. Through a communication made on Thursday to our contemporary the *Globe*, it became known that a Chinese visitor to England, a doctor named Sun Yat Sen, was imprisoned at the house of the Chinese Minister, and that it was supposed to be the intention of his captors to send him under restraint to his own country, there to receive such measure of justice as a Chinese tribunal might be expected to extend to an alleged conspirator. Fortunately for the prisoner, he had studied medicine at Hong Kong, where he had made the acquaintance and had won the friendly regard of Mr. Cantlie, the Dean of the Hong Kong Medical College, and of Dr. Manson, both of whom are now residing in London. Sun Yat Sen was sufficiently supplied with money, and he succeeded in finding means of communication with these English friends, who at once took steps to inform the police authorities and the Foreign Office of what was being done, while, at the same time, they employed detectives to watch the Legation, in order to prevent the possibility of the prisoner being secretly conveyed away. Lord Salisbury, as soon as he was informed of what had occurred, made a demand for the immediate release of the prisoner, who was forthwith set at liberty, and was taken away by Mr. Cantlie and Dr. Manson, who attended in order to identify him as the person they had known. He has since furnished representatives of the Press with an account of the circumstances of his capture and detention, an account which differs in important respects from that of the Chinese authorities. If the Chinese had accomplished their supposed object, and had smuggled Sun Yat Sen on shipboard, to be tried and probably executed in China, our Foreign Office would have had to deal with an offence against the comity of nations for which it would have been necessary to demand and obtain the punishment of all concerned. The failure of the attempt may perhaps be held to bring it too near the confines of comic opera to furnish a subject for anything more than serious remonstrance.

The offence alleged against Sun Yat Sen is that his medical character is a mere cloak for other designs, and that he is really Sun Wên, the prime mover in a conspiracy which was discovered in 1894, and which had for its object the dethronement of the present reigning dynasty. The first step of the conspirators was to be the capture of the Viceroy of Canton, who was to be kidnapped when inspecting the arsenal; but the plot, like most plots, leaked out or was betrayed, and fifteen of the ringleaders were arrested and decapitated. Sun Wên saved himself by timely flight, and made his way through Honolulu and America to this country, being all the time carefully watched by detectives. On reaching England, at the beginning of the present month, he called upon his old friends, Mr. Cantlie and Dr. Manson, and prepared to commence a course of medical study in London. A few days later he disappeared, and on the evening of last Saturday Mr. Cantlie was informed of his position. Sun Wên, or Sun Yat Sen, whichever he may be alleges that he was walking in or near Portland Place on the 11th inst., when he was accosted in the street by a fellow-countryman, who asked whether he was Chinese or Japanese; and, being told in reply that he was Chinese and a native of Canton, hailed him as a fellow provincial, and kept him in conversation until a second and then a third Chinaman joined them. One of the three left, while the other two walked slowly on until they reached the Legation, when the others invited Sun to enter, and supported the invitation by the exercise of a certain amount of force. As soon as he was inside, the door was shut and he was conveyed upstairs to a room where, as he alleges, he was seen by Sir Halliday Macartney, and in which he was afterwards kept close prisoner until released by the intervention of Lord Salisbury. The officials of the Chinese Legation, on the other hand, assert that the man came to the Legation of his own accord on Saturday, the 10th, and entered into conversation, talking about Chinese affairs, and appearing to want only a chat with some of his fellow-countrymen, after having which he went away; and that it was not until after he had gone that suspicion was excited that he might be the notorious Sun Wên, who had fled from justice at home, whose passage through America and departure for England had already been telegraphed to the Legation, and who was actually then being watched by a private detective in the employment of the Chinese Government.

Sun came to the Legation a second time, on Sunday, the 11th, and then, evidence of his identity having been obtained, he was made prisoner. It had been supposed that he was about to return to Hong Kong as to a convenient base for further operations; and it was the intention of the Chinese Government to ask for his extradition as soon as he arrived there. In the meanwhile the actual presence of the supposed conspirator in the Legation furnished a temptation which it was found impossible to resist, and he was locked up until instructions with regard to him could arrive from Pekin. There can be little doubt that these instructions, if they had been received and could have been acted upon, would have effectually destroyed his power to engage in any further conspiracies; and it may be assumed that the intervention of Lord Salisbury was not too early. Even as it was Sun appears to have suffered considerable anxiety lest the food supplied to him at the Legation should be unwholesome in its character.

The simple process of cutting a knot is often preferable to the labour of untying it, and we are not very much surprised that the Chinese Minister or his representative should have authorized the adoption of the course which has happily failed of success. But we cannot conceal our surprise that Sir Halliday Macartney, himself an Englishman, should have taken any part in a transaction manifestly doomed to failure, and the success of which would have been ruinous to all engaged in it. The Chinese Minister is said to have surrendered his prisoner "without prejudice," as lawyers say, to his assumed rights; but he appears to have claimed a right which is not acknowledged by any civilized country, and which would be intolerable if it were exercised. It would be a somewhat similar proceeding if the Turkish Ambassador were to inveigle some of the leading members of the Armenian colony in London into the Embassy, in order to despatch them, gagged and bound, as an offering to his Imperial Majesty the Sultan, or if Lord Dufferin had in the same way made a private prisoner of Tynan, and had sent him to stand his trial at the Old Bailey. It is well recognised that the house of a foreign mission is regarded as a portion of the country from which the mission is sent, and that not only the Minister himself, but also the recognised members of his suite, enjoy an immunity from liability to the laws of the country to which the Ambassador is accredited; but this hardly entitles the Ambassador to exercise powers of imprisonment or of criminal jurisdiction, and the privileges of the Embassy as a place of refuge for persons unconnected with it are strictly limited to the ground on which it stands. Even if the Chinese Minister could not have been prevented from keeping Sun in custody, he would have been liberated by the police as soon as he was brought over the threshold to be conveyed elsewhere. It is fortunate that he did not suffer from any form

of illness; for if he had died during his imprisonment, it is very difficult to say what could have
been done in consequence. Evidence would have
been very hard to procure; and, even if it had
been procured, the persons of the Minister and of
his servants would have been sacred. Probably
the only course would have been to demand that
the Minister should be recalled, and that he should
be put upon his trial in his own country; a demand
which might perhaps have been readily complied
with, but which might not improbably have led to
what Englishmen would describe as a miscarriage
of justice. We think that this country, almost as
much as the prisoner, may be congratulated upon
the turn of events; and we have no doubt that
the Foreign Office will find ways and means of
making the rulers of the Celestial Empire understand that they have gone a little too far, and that
they must not commit any similar offence in the
future.

This Article called forth a remonstrance
from Sir Halliday Macartney, in which
he stated his views:

To the Editor of THE TIMES.

SIR,—In your leading article of to-day, com-
menting on the alleged kidnapping of an individ-
ual, a Chinese subject, calling himself, amongst
numerous other aliases, by the name of Sun Yat
Sen, you make some remarks with regard to me

which I cannot but consider as an exception to the fairness which in general characterises the comments of *The Times*.

After stating the case as given by the two opposite parties, in the surprise which you express at my conduct, you take it for granted that the statement of Sun Yat Sen is the correct one and that of the Chinese Legation the wrong one.

I do not know why you make this assumption, for you undoubtedly do so when you say the case is as if the Turkish Ambassador had inveigled some of the members of the Armenian colony of London into the Embassy with a view to making them a present to his Majesty the Sultan.

Now, I repeat what I have said before—that in this case there was no inveiglement. The statement of Sun Yat Sen—or, to call him by his real name, Sun Wên—that he was caught in the street and hustled into the Legation by two sturdy Chinamen is utterly false.

He came to the Legation unexpectedly and of his own accord, the first time on Saturday, the 10th, the second on Sunday, the 11th.

Whatever the pundits of international law may think of his detention, they may take it as being absolutely certain that there was no kidnapping and that he entered the Legation without the employment of force or guile.

I am, Sir, your obedient servant,

HALLIDAY MACARTNEY.

Richmond House,
49 Portland Place, W.,
Oct. 24th.

Sir Halliday Macartney's remarks about my going under various aliases, is no doubt intended to cast a slur upon my character; but Sir Halliday knows, no one better, that every Chinaman has four names at least to which he is entitled. 1st, the name one's parents bestow on their child. 2nd, the name given by the schoolmaster. 3rd, the name a young man wishes to be known by when he goes out into society. 4th, the name he takes when he is married. The only constant part of the name is the first syllable— the surname, really the family name, the other part of the name varies according as it is the parent, the schoolmaster etc., chooses. Whilst upon this subject it may not be without interest to know that my accuser has various aliases by which he is known to the Chinese. In addition to the name Ma-Ta-Yen, which means Macartney, His Excellency, he is also known as Ma-Ka-Ni, and as Ma-Tsing-

Shan, showing that no name is constant in China except the family name.

From THE SPEAKER, *October 31st, 1896.*

THE DUNGEONS OF PORTLAND PLACE.

Sir Halliday Macartney is an official in the service of the Chinese Government. That fact seems to have deprived him of any sense of humour he might otherwise have had, which, we imagine, would in no circumstances have been conspicuous. The Secretary of the Chinese Legation has struck an attitude of injured innocence in *The Times.* He is like Woods Pasha, when that undiscerning personage stands up for the Turkish Government in an English newspaper. What in a true Oriental would seem natural and characteristic, in the sham Oriental is merely ridiculous. Sir Halliday Macartney assures the world that the Chinese medical gentleman who was lately released from the Portland Place Bastille was not inveigled into that institution. To the obvious suggestion that Sun Yat Sen would never have walked into the Chinese Embassy of his own accord, had he known the real identity of his entertainers, Sir Halliday vouchsafes no reply. It is unquestionable that he saw the captive, and took no measures to set him at liberty, till a peremptory requisition came from the Foreign Office. If it was not intended to

9

deport Sun Yat Sen to China, why was he kept a prisoner ?   Sir Halliday Macartney is in the pitiable position of an Englishman who is forced by his official obligations to palliate in London what would be the ordinary course of justice at Canton. A purely Chinese emissary would have said nothing. Having failed in his manœuvre, he would have accepted the consequences of defeat with the fatalism of his race and native climate. The spectacle of Sir Halliday Macartney fussing and fuming in the *Times* like an Englishman, when he ought to hold his peace like a Chinaman, can only suggest to the authorities at Pekin that their English representative here is a rather incompetent person.

On the other hand, there is something in this Chinese kidnapping which is irresistibly diverting. Englishmen can never take the Chinaman seriously, in spite of Charles Pearson's prediction that the yellow man will one day eat us up. The personality of Ah Sin, especially when he wears a pigtail and his native costume, is purely comic to the average sightseer. If the men who decoyed Sun Yat Sen were pointed out to a London crowd, they would be greeted not with indignation, but with mildly derisive banter. It might go hard with any Europeans who had tried the same game; but Ah Sin, the childlike and bland, is a traditional joke. His strategy excites no more resentment than the nodding of the ornamental mandarin on the mantelpiece. The popular idea of Lord Salisbury's intervention in this case is probably that the Chinaman's pigtail has been gently but decisively pulled, and that such a lesson is quite sufficient without any public anger. Had a German or a Frenchman been kidnapped in similar circumstances, the situation would at once have been recognised as extremely serious. The capture and incarceration in Portland Place simply excite a smile. The newspapers have treated the incident as they treat the announcement that Li Hung Chang, promoted to be Imperial Chancellor of China, had at the same time been punished for an unauthorised visit to the Empress Dowager. How can you be angry with a people whose solemnities frequently strike the Occidental mind as screaming farce? It is impossible to pass No. 40 Portland Place with a romantic shudder. That middle-class dwelling, of substantial and comfortable aspect, is now a Bastille *pour rire*, and excites the mirth of tradesmen's boys, who must feel strongly tempted, by way of celebrating the Fifth of November, to ring the bell and introduce a Celestial guy to the puzzled servitors of the Embassy, with a fluent tirade in pigeon-English.

As for Sun Yat Sen, it cannot escape his notice that there is little curiosity to know the precise reason why he is obnoxious to the Chinese Government. He is said to have taken part in a conspiracy against the Viceroy of Canton, a statement which conveys no vivid impression to the popular mind. Political refugees—Italians, Poles, Hungarians—have commonly inspired a romantic interest in this country. They have figured in our fiction, always a sure criterion of public sympathies. When the storyteller takes the foreign conspirator in hand, you may be sure that the machinations, escapes, and so forth touch a responsive chord in the popular imagination. But no storyteller is likely to turn the adventures of Sun Yat Sen to such account, though they may be really thrilling, and though this worthy Celestial medico may have been quite a formidable person in his native land. Even the realistic descriptions by travellers of Chinese administration, the gentle coercion of witnesses in the courts by smashing their ankles, the slicing of criminals to death, have not given a sinister background to the figure of the Heathen Chinee. The ignominious defeat of the Chinese arms in the late war has strengthened the conception of the yellow man as a rather grotesquely ineffectual object. If Sun Yat Sen were to deliver a lecture on his adventures, and paint the tyranny of the Viceroy of Canton in the deepest colours, or if Sir Halliday Macartney were to show that his late prisoner was a monster of ferocity, compared to whom all the Western dynamiters were angels in disguise, we doubt whether either story would command the gravity of the public. The Chinese have their virtues; they are a frugal, thrifty, and abstemious people; they practise a greater respect for family ties than Western nations. The custom of worshipping their ancestors, though one of the chief stumbling-blocks to the Christian missionaries, probably exercises a greater moral influence than the reverence for genealogy here. But no audience in England or America would accept these virtues as rebukes to the short-comings of the Anglo-Saxon civilisation. So deep is the gulf between Occident and Orient that the pride of neither will learn from the other, and both are indifferent to the warnings of prophets who foretell the triumph of the Caucasian in the Flowery Land or the submergement of Europe by the yellow flood of immigration. All Western notions are regarded in China with a contempt which even the travels of Li are not likely to dispel; and No. 40 Portland Place can never recover that prestige of harmless nonentity it enjoyed before the pranks of the Chinese Embassy made it a centre of the ludicrous.

The following is a copy of the letter I sent to the newspapers thanking the Government and the Press for what they had done for me:

To the Editor of the ———

SIR,—Will you kindly express through your columns my keen appreciation of the action of the British Government in effecting my release from the Chinese Legation? I have also to thank the Press generally for their timely help and sympathy. If anything were needed to convince me of the generous public spirit which pervades Great Britain, and the love of justice which distinguishes its people, the recent acts of the last few days have conclusively done so.

Knowing and feeling more keenly than ever what a constitutional Government and an enlightened people mean, I am prompted still more actively to pursue the cause of advancement, education, and civilisation in my own well-beloved but oppressed country.

Yours faithfully,

SUN YAT SEN.

46 Devonshire Street,
   Portland Place, W.,
     Oct. 24.

THE END.

PRINTING OFFICE OF THE PUBLISHER.

Arrowsmith's 3/6 Series.

Crown 8vo, cloth.

Bristol: J. W. ARROWSMITH, 11 Quay Street.
London: SIMPKIN, MARSHALL, HAMILTON, KENT & CO. LIMITED.

Arrowsmith's Bristol Library.

Fcap. 8vo, stiff covers, 1/-; cloth, 1/6.

Saturday Review speaks of ARROWSMITH'S BRISTOL LIBRARY "as necessary to the traveller as a rug in winter and a dust-coat in summer."

Arrowsmith's Bristol Library.

Fcap. 8vo, stiff covers, 1/-; cloth, 1/6.

"Mr. Arrowsmith, since the far-off days when he discovered poor Hugh Conway, has made the public his debtors for many a delightful book."—*Liverpool Post.*

40.	HARD LUCK.	ARTHUR À BECKETT.
41.	TWO AND TWO. A Tale of Four .	ELIZABETH GLAISTER.
42.	THE RAJAH AND THE ROSEBUD	WILLIAM SIME.
43.	BEHIND THE KAFES	MARY ALBERT.
44.	THE DEMONIAC	WALTER BESANT.
45.	OUR BOYS & GIRLS AT SCHOOL.	HENRY J. BARKER, B.A.
46.	THE CORONER'S UNDERSTUDY .	CAPTAIN COE.
47.	A ROMANCE OF THE MOORS .	MONA CAIRD.
48.	THE SHIELD OF LOVE	B. L. FARJEON.
49.	A SPINSTER'S DIARY	Mrs. A. PHILLIPS.
50.	THE AVENGING OF HIRAM	BENNETT COLL.
51.	TRAVELLERS' TALES . .	Edited by E. A. MORTON.
52.	THE GREAT SHADOW . .	A. CONAN DOYLE.
53.	HARRY FORRESTER, late Blankth	{ ANNIE THOMAS (Mrs. Pender-Cudlip)
54.	{ A GEM OF CREMONA . { A CHEF D'ŒUVRE	B. M. VERE and E. BLAIR-OLIPHANT.
55.	THE SLAPPING SAL and OTHER TALES	{ A. CONAN DOYLE. { VARIOUS AUTHORS.
56.	DECEMBER ROSES	Mrs. CAMPBELL PRAED.
57.	THE TRESPASSER	GILBERT PARKER.
58.	THE TELEPORON and OTHER STORIES	} W. H. STACPOOLE.
59.	AT THE SIGN OF THE WICKET .	E. B. V. CHRISTIAN.
60.	CONSCIENCE MAKES THE MARTYR	} S. M. CRAWLEY-BOEVEY.
61.	AN UNFINISHED MARTYRDOM and OTHER STORIES . . .	} A. ST. JOHN ADCOCK.
62.	THE INDISCRETION OF THE DUCHESS . . .	} ANTHONY HOPE.
63.	AN APOSTLE OF FREEDOM	EDWIN HUGHES, B.A.
64.	ENGLAND v. AUSTRALIA	J. N. PENTELOW.
65.	THE ADVENTURES OF ARTHUR ROBERTS, by Road, Rail, and River	{ TOLD BY HIMSELF, and chronicled by RICHARD MORTON.
66.	IN THE SMOKE OF WAR . .	WALTER RAYMOND.
67.	PENLEY ON HIMSELF.	
68.	TOLD IN THE PAVILION . .	ALFRED COCHRANE.
69.	HOW 'S THAT? Including "A Century of Grace." Verses. Cricket Sketches.	} HARRY FURNISS. E. J. MILLIKEN. E. B. V. CHRISTIAN.
70.	MY TERRIBLE TWIN . . .	FRED WHISHAW.
71.	THE RECOVERY OF JANE VERCOE and OTHER STORIES . . .	} MABEL QUILLER-COUCH.
72.	THE WIZARD	RIDER H. HAGGARD.